CRCS Prep with Practice Questions for the AAHAM Certified Revenue Cycle Specialist Institutional and Professional Exams
[2nd Edition]

Matthew Lanni

Copyright © 2021 by APEX Publishing

All rights reserved. This book or any portion thereof may not be reproduced or used in any manner whatsoever without the express written permission of the publisher except for the use of brief quotations in a book review.

Written and edited by APEX Publishing.

ISBN 13: 9781637753590
ISBN 10: 1637753594

APEX Publishing is not connected with or endorsed by any official testing organization. APEX Publishing creates and publishes unofficial educational products. All test and organization names are trademarks of their respective owners.

The material in this publication is included for utilitarian purposes only and does not constitute an endorsement by APEX Publishing of any particular point of view.

Table of Contents

Test Taking Strategies 1
Introduction to the Certified Revenue Cycle Specialist (CRCS-I/CRCS-P) Exam 4
CRCS General Test Tips 6
Federal Regulations and Governing Bodies 7
Patient Access Services 12
Hospital and Clinic Billing 17
Credit and Collections 26
Practice Questions 30
Answer Explanations 31

Test Taking Strategies

1. Reading the Whole Question

A popular assumption in Western culture is the idea that we don't have enough time for anything. We speed while driving to work, we want to read an assignment for class as quickly as possible, or we want the line in the supermarket to dwindle faster. However, speeding through such events robs us from being able to thoroughly appreciate and understand what's happening around us. While taking a timed test, the feeling one might have while reading a question is to find the correct answer as quickly as possible. Although pace is important, don't let it deter you from reading the whole question. Test writers know how to subtly change a test question toward the end in various ways, such as adding a negative or changing focus. If the question has a passage, carefully read the whole passage as well before moving on to the questions. This will help you process the information in the passage rather than worrying about the questions you've just read and where to find them. A thorough understanding of the passage or question is an important way for test takers to be able to succeed on an exam.

2. Examining Every Answer Choice

Let's say we're at the market buying apples. The first apple we see on top of the heap may *look* like the best apple, but if we turn it over we can see bruising on the skin. We must examine several apples before deciding which apple is the best. Finding the correct answer choice is like finding the best apple. Although it's tempting to choose an answer that seems correct at first without reading the others, it's important to read each answer choice thoroughly before making a final decision on the answer. The aim of a test writer might be to get as close as possible to the correct answer, so watch out for subtle words that may indicate an answer is incorrect. Once the correct answer choice is selected, read the question again and the answer in response to make sure all your bases are covered.

3. Eliminating Wrong Answer Choices

Sometimes we become paralyzed when we are confronted with too many choices. Which frozen yogurt flavor is the tastiest? Which pair of shoes look the best with this outfit? What type of car will fill my needs as a consumer? If you are unsure of which answer would be the best to choose, it may help to use process of elimination. We use "filtering" all the time on sites such as eBay® or Craigslist® to eliminate the ads that are not right for us. We can do the same thing on an exam. Process of elimination is crossing out the answer choices we know for sure are wrong and leaving the ones that might be correct. It may help to cover up the incorrect answer choice. Covering incorrect choices is a psychological act that alleviates stress due to the brain being exposed to a smaller amount of information. Choosing between two answer choices is much easier than choosing between all of them, and you have a better chance of selecting the correct answer if you have less to focus on.

4. Sticking to the World of the Question

When we are attempting to answer questions, our minds will often wander away from the question and what it is asking. We begin to see answer choices that are true in the real world instead of true in the world of the question. It may be helpful to think of each test question as its own little world. This world may be different from ours. This world may know as a truth that the chicken came before the egg or may assert that two plus two equals five. Remember that, no matter what hypothetical nonsense may be in the question, assume it to be true. If the question states that the chicken came before the egg, then choose your answer based on that truth. Sticking to the world of the question means placing all of our biases and assumptions aside and relying on the question to guide us to the correct answer. If we are simply looking for answers that are correct based on our own judgment, then we may choose incorrectly. Remember an answer that is true does not necessarily answer the question.

5. Key Words

If you come across a complex test question that you have to read over and over again, try pulling out some key words from the question in order to understand what exactly it is asking. Key words may be words that surround the question, such as *main idea, analogous, parallel, resembles, structured,* or *defines*. The question may be asking for the main idea, or it may be asking you to define something. Deconstructing the sentence may also be helpful in making the question simpler before trying to answer it. This means taking the sentence apart and obtaining meaning in pieces, or separating the question from the foundation of the question. For example, let's look at this question:

> Given the author's description of the content of paleontology in the first paragraph, which of the following is most parallel to what it taught?

The question asks which one of the answers most *parallels* the following information: The *description* of paleontology in the first paragraph. The first step would be to see *how* paleontology is described in the first paragraph. Then, we would find an answer choice that parallels that description. The question seems complex at first, but after we deconstruct it, the answer becomes much more attainable.

6. Subtle Negatives

Negative words in question stems will be words such as *not, but, neither,* or *except*. Test writers often use these words in order to trick unsuspecting test takers into selecting the wrong answer—or, at least, to test their reading comprehension of the question. Many exams will feature the negative words in all caps (*which of the following is NOT an example*), but some questions will add the negative word seamlessly into the sentence. The following is an example of a subtle negative used in a question stem:

> According to the passage, which of the following is *not* considered to be an example of paleontology?

If we rush through the exam, we might skip that tiny word, *not*, inside the question, and choose an answer that is opposite of the correct choice. Again, it's important to read the question fully, and double check for any words that may negate the statement in any way.

7. Spotting the Hedges

The word "hedging" refers to language that remains vague or avoids absolute terminology. Absolute terminology consists of words like *always, never, all, every, just, only, none,* and *must*. Hedging refers to words like *seem, tend, might, most, some, sometimes, perhaps, possibly, probability,* and *often*. In some cases, we want to choose answer choices that use hedging and avoid answer choices that use absolute terminology. It's important to pay attention to what subject you are on and adjust your response accordingly.

8. Restating to Understand

Every now and then we come across questions that we don't understand. The language may be too complex, or the question is structured in a way that is meant to confuse the test taker. When you come across a question like this, it may be worth your time to rewrite or restate the question in your own words in order to understand it better. For example, let's look at the following complicated question:

> Which of the following words, if substituted for the word *parochial* in the first paragraph, would LEAST change the meaning of the sentence?

Let's restate the question in order to understand it better. We know that they want the word *parochial* replaced. We also know that this new word would "least" or "not" change the meaning of the sentence. Now let's try the sentence again:

> Which word could we replace with *parochial*, and it would not change the meaning?

Restating it this way, we see that the question is asking for a synonym. Now, let's restate the question so we can answer it better:

> Which word is a synonym for the word *parochial*?

Before we even look at the answer choices, we have a simpler, restated version of a complicated question.

9. Predicting the Answer

After you read the question, try predicting the answer *before* reading the answer choices. By formulating an answer in your mind, you will be less likely to be distracted by any wrong answer choices. Using predictions will also help you feel more confident in the answer choice you select. Once you've chosen your answer, go back and reread the question and answer choices to make sure you have the best fit. If you have no idea what the answer may be for a particular question, forego using this strategy.

10. Avoiding Patterns

One popular myth in grade school relating to standardized testing is that test writers will often put multiple-choice answers in patterns. A runoff example of this kind of thinking is that the most common answer choice is "C," with "B" following close behind. Or, some will advocate certain made-up word patterns that simply do not exist. Test writers do not arrange their correct answer choices in any kind of pattern; their choices are randomized. There may even be times where the correct answer choice will be the same letter for two or three questions in a row, but we have no way of knowing when or if this might happen. Instead of trying to figure out what choice the test writer probably set as being correct, focus on what the *best answer choice* would be out of the answers you are presented with. Use the tips above, general knowledge, and reading comprehension skills in order to best answer the question, rather than looking for patterns that do not exist.

Introduction to the Certified Revenue Cycle Specialist (CRCS-I/CRCS-P) Exam

The CRCS exams are required for individuals seeking the American Association of Healthcare Administration Management (AAHAM) certification as a Certified Revenue Cycle Specialist. Achieving certification can afford candidates recognition in the industry, commitment to and proficiency in the job, and can be an important step in career growth and advancement because it confirms one's knowledge and expertise in job-specific skills related to the revenue cycle. Test takers must have a command of current Medicare guidelines and deductibles and will encounter exam questions that address the most current standards and changes in the industry.

The more appropriate CRCS exam—either the CRCS-I or CRCS-P—for an individual depends on the side of the revenue cycle their work duties primarily fall. Those who work on the hospital or health system side should take the institutional version, the CRCS-I. Those who have primary responsibilities on the clinic or physician side should take the professional version, the CRCS-P.

Although not required to sit for the exam or earn certification, AAHAM membership is encouraged to all prospective CRCS candidates. Individuals eligible to take either the CRCS-I or CRCS-P exams are those whose roles involve the managing of patients' healthcare accounts. The AAHAM recommends that test takers have at least one year of employment experience in patient accounting prior to attempting the exam.

Test Administration

The CRCS exams are offered three times a year. The available testing dates are usually in the second half of the months of March, July, and November. Candidates should refer to their local AAHAM for exact dates, times, and locations of the administration of the exam.

It is important to note that there are deadlines for applying for the CRCS exams. Candidates wanting to take either exam in March must submit their application early enough that the AAHAM National Office receives it by mid-December of the previous year. The deadline for the July exam is in April, and the deadline for the November exam is in August. Interested candidates should refer to the AAHAM website for the exact dates (aaham.org). Accepted test candidates will receive an exam confirmation email from their local Chapter Certification Chair with the date, time, and location of their exam and the name of the proctor.

The CRCS is administered online under the supervision of a proctor. Retakes are permitted. Test takers who pass two of the three sections of the exam may retake just the one missed section. However, if a test taker does not pass two sections during a single attempt at the exam, the entire exam (all three sections) must be retaken, even the section that was previously passed. Any retakes on a single section must be attempted and passed within twelve months of the candidate's original test date.

Test Format

The CRCS exams have three sections: patient access, billing, and credit and collections for the CRCS-I and front desk, billing, and credit and collections for the CRCS-P. Each section contains 40 multiple-choice questions that address various aspects of the revenue cycle, including current regulations, policies, and

acronyms. When attempting the entire exam, candidate are afforded two hours. The time drops to 80 minutes for two sections and 40 minutes for one section.

Test takers who already hold either the CRCS-I or CRCS-P certification can take an 80-minute exam, consisting of two sections, to obtain dual certification. Both sections must be passed in one single testing attempt; otherwise, a retest of both sections is required.

Scoring

A score of 70% or higher on all three sections of the exam is required to obtain a passing score. Immediately upon completion and submission of the exam, test takers will receive notification of their passing status. Those test takers who successfully pass the exam will receive a mailed certification by the end of the month after the period in which they took the exam.

CRCS General Test Tips

While the bulk of any CRCS candidate's exam preparation will come in the form of their years of experience on the job, there are some additional strategies and test-taking tips that can help ensure a smooth test day and the achievement of one's maximal score. The following tips and strategies are useful in the preparation and testing process of the CRCS exam:

Contact your local AAHAM chapter and inquire about the availability of coaching sessions. These sessions, which are offered by most chapters, provide one of the best environments to get questions answered, receive the latest updates on content that will be tested, and find out details about the exam. AAHAM professionals want CRCS candidates to succeed and pass the exam, so they are invested in making these coaching sessions as productive and helpful as possible.

Find a study partner. Contacting your local chapter can be one way to find someone else planning to take the exam when you are. Attending the coaching sessions is another avenue by which study partners can be found. Working together can improve scores by allowing each person to share their strengths with the other person and clarify points of confusion.

Know the current Medicare rules and regulations backward and forward. This includes the specific deductibles and coinsurance amounts, particularly for Part A and Part B, for each major type of service. Medicare is one of the largest payers; accordingly, it makes up a significant portion of the exam.

Practice "thinking" in acronyms. In many cases, questions will only refer to an organization, law, or policy by its acronym. The full name will not be used. For example, instead of seeing the words "The Healthcare Fraud Prevention and Enforcement Action Team" on the exam, you might only encounter the acronym HEAT. It is critical to study the acronyms along with the full name. Because the exam has a time limit, it will behoove you to save time wherever possible so that it can be banked and applied to difficult questions.

Memorize the HICN suffixes. Although they are numerous, HICN suffixes are nearly guaranteed to be on the exam. You can nail all of those questions by memorizing the suffixes. Flash cards can be a particularly useful study tool for augmenting rote memorization.

Arrive to the testing center at least 15 minutes early. Budget extra time to get there so that you can park, register, use the facilities, and get yourself mentally ready to focus without the stress of running behind. You will not be permitted to sit for the exam if you arrive late.

Be confident. If you have studied well, there's no reason to be overly intimidated by the exam. You will perform better if you are relaxed and feeling capable.

Federal Regulations and Governing Bodies

Federal Agencies that Have a Significant Role in Healthcare

The Department of Health and Human Services (HHS)
A cabinet-level department of the federal government, the **Department of Health and Human Services** (DHHS, or just HHS), strives to protect the health, safety, and wellbeing of all Americans by providing necessary health-related services, especially to those with limited ability to help themselves. It was founded in 1939 and has added programs and divisions over the years to better serve Americans.

HHS Programs
Across all eleven of its operating divisions, HHS administers over 115 programs, including programs related to social services, maintaining healthcare privacy, preparing for disasters, and advancing health research. Additionally, HHS offers many educational resources and tools to the public regarding relevant health information, such as disease prevention, links to healthcare facilities and providers, wellness screenings, and information about health insurance. There are programs that provide financial assistance to those with low incomes, programs designed to foster better maternal and infant health, Medicare and Medicaid, immunization and other disease prevention programs, and food delivery programs for home-bound elderly individuals, among many others.

HHS Operating Divisions
HHS has eight public health services agencies and three human service agencies for a total of eleven operating divisions. Of these, the ones most applicable to health services include the following:

- Agency for Healthcare Research and Quality
- Agency for Toxic Substances and Disease Registry
- Centers for Disease Control and Prevention
- Centers for Medicare & Medicaid Services
- Food and Drug Administration
- Health Resources and Services Administration
- Indian Health Service
- National Institutes of Health
- Substance Abuse and Mental Health Services Administration

Centers for Medicare and Medicaid Services (CMS)
A division of HSS, **Centers for Medicare and Medicaid Services** (CMS) administers the Medicare program. It also works with state governments to administer the Medicaid program, the Children's Health Insurance Program, and portability standards for health insurance in general. Additionally, CMS has roles in administering simplified HIPAA standards, surveying and certifying standards for nursing home care and clinical laboratories, and overseeing the website HealthCare.gov.

CMS Mission
The **mission of CMS** is to listen to and heed to the needs of the populations they serve and to ensure the programs and policies run by the agency are constantly developing and being evaluated and implemented in the most effective ways. Equal access to the best healthcare services and healthcare security for all beneficiaries is a key component of CMS's mission. The agency's vision is that all their beneficiaries reach their best health level, and that all healthcare quality and access disparities are eliminated.

Quality Improvement Organization (QIO) Program
The purpose of the **Quality Improvement Organization (QIO) Program** is to improve the effectiveness, efficiency, and quality of services delivered to Medicare beneficiaries at a lower cost. In its goal of providing better healthcare at a lower cost to the populations served, the QIO Program ensures that Medicare only covers necessary and reasonable goods and services. The program also ensures that beneficiaries are protected by efficiently addressing complaints, such as those from individual beneficiaries and providers.

General Provisions of Healthcare-Related Federal Regulations

The Patient Bill of Rights' Goals and Guarantees
The **Patient Bill of Rights**, established in 1998, aims to ensure the healthcare system meets patients' needs, maintains fairness, and emphasizes the importance of the relationship between patients and their providers and the pivotal role patients have in maintaining good health.

Right to Privacy and Security of Health Information
Patients have a right to confidentiality of their health information. Healthcare information should be protected, and conversations between healthcare providers and patients are to be private. Patients have a right to receive a copy of their health records and ask for corrections.

The Privacy Act of 1974 set guidelines for what personal information can be maintained by federal agencies. This act states that all persons must give consent before their records within the system are released to any third party. There are exceptions to this rule, such as for statistical purposes, law enforcement purposes, or congressional investigations, among others.

The Health Insurance Portability and Accountability Act (HIPAA) of 1996 was enacted to set standards regarding the use and disclosure of protected health information, the privacy rights of patients, and patients' rights to control how their health information is used. One of the main goals is to allow protected health information to remain private and secure, while still allowing proper treatment through effective communication between providers regarding the patient's health.

Right to Participate in Treatment Decisions
Patients have the right to participate in decisions regarding their healthcare treatment or have a designated guardian or representative perform this role should they need assistance.

The Patient Self Determination Act (PSDA) of 1990 is designed to ensure patients understand their right to be involved in decisions regarding their personal healthcare. Information concerning advanced directives must be made available by medical providers and hospitals.

An **advance directive** is a document that grants permission to someone else should the individual to whom it pertains become unable to make their own healthcare decisions. Do Not Resuscitate (DNR) orders, organ and tissue donation decisions, and the use of dialysis or ventilators are examples of things that may be included on an advanced directive. A Living Will and a Durable Power of Attorney for Healthcare are the most common types.

Affordable Care
The Affordable Care Act (ACA)
The Affordable Care Act was enacted in March of 2010. Sometimes called *Obamacare*, the law aims to increase the number of people for whom health insurance is affordable, particularly via subsidies to those

with household incomes between 100 to 400% of the federal poverty level. It also aims to expand Medicaid to cover adults who have incomes that fall below 138% of the federal poverty level. Overall, the act helps to develop healthcare delivery methods that are affordable and reduce healthcare costs.

Implementation for Tax-Exempt Hospitals

Tax-exempt hospitals must satisfy certain requirements per the ACA to retain their tax status. For example, they must have written policies regarding financial assistance and emergency medical care that limit the financial responsibility for emergency or other medically-necessary care to patients eligible for financial assistance. They must also work with patients to determine their eligibility for financial assistance before sending any unfulfilled charges to collections, and conduct and implement a CHNA at least once every three years. Failing to abide by these regulations, and others imposed based on the ACA, will result in a tax penalty.

Consumer Marketplace

The **Marketplace** is a service operated by the U.S. government at healthcare.gov that helps Americans learn about, compare, and enroll in affordable health insurance either online, via phone, or in person. Some states run similar marketplaces.

In addition to the Marketplace on HealthCare.gov or marketplaces operated by individual states, consumers can also learn about available health insurance options through websites dedicated to various insurance plans or through their employer if healthcare is a benefit. There are also designated agents and brokers who can help make coverage recommendations.

Anti-Fraud and Abuse

Tactics to reduce healthcare and health insurance fraud and abuse are critical because these illegal acts cost private health insurance companies, as well as Medicare and Medicaid, billions of dollars per year.

Fraud Versus Abuse: **Fraud** is intentionally deceiving or misrepresenting services that could yield an unauthorized reimbursement to a healthcare practice. **Abuse** is engaging in activities that are considered inconsistent with those accepted by the industry as sound medical, business, or financial practice. Fraud is more serious than abuse and can result in criminal charges.

The False Claims Act: The federal government's civil tool in fraud situations involving the Medicare and Medicaid programs is the False Claims Act (FCA). Under this statute, it is illegal for an individual to deliberately submit a fraudulent claim or one with a false statement to the federal government.

CMS Administrative Sanctions: The CMS Administrative Sanctions says that the Office of Inspector General (OIG) can inflict Civil Monetary Payments, exclusions, and other administrative actions on providers who commit fraud or abuse with any federal or state health program.

The Criminal Healthcare Fraud Statute: Under the Criminal Healthcare Fraud Statute, the Department of Justice (DOJ) can hold an individual liable for knowingly and deliberately defrauding any program related to healthcare benefits or for providing false statements to receive payments from Medicare or Medicaid. Doing so can result in significant fines and prison time of up to ten years.

Exclusions by the Office of Inspector General (OIG): The Office of Inspector General is permitted to exclude individuals and groups from Medicare, Medicaid, and other federally-funded healthcare programs. Those with criminal charges and who have committed fraud are among those OIG will exclude.

Healthcare Fraud Prevention and Enforcement Action Team (HEAT): HEAT is a joint initiative between HHS, OIG, and the DOJ intended to fight healthcare fraud. One of the key aspects of the program is the Medicare Fraud Strike Force team, which aims to catch, stop, and punish emerging fraudulent schemes.

Credit and Collections

The following acts are designed to protect consumers against unfair credit and collections actions.

Truth in Lending Act: Passed in 1968, the Truth in Lending Act is a federal law intended to protect consumers and ensure businesses in the lending marketplace treat consumers fairly and are transparent about the true cost of credit. For example, lending companies must disclose credit terms, interest rates, fees, and conditions in common language.

Fair Credit Billing Act: The Fair Credit Billing Act was enacted in 1974 as an amendment to the Truth in Lending Act to protect consumers against unjust billing issues and errors, such as charges for damaged goods, unauthorized charges, charges of the wrong amount, etc.

Fair Credit Reporting Act: The Fair Credit Reporting Act was enacted in 1970. The purpose of this act is to protect consumers from intentional or negligent inclusion of incorrect information on their credit reports and to regulate the use of consumers' information.

Fair Debt Collection Practices Act: The Fair Debt Collection Practices Act protects consumers against debt collection practices that are abusive or unjust and gives them methods by which they can dispute debt.

Equal Credit Opportunity Act: The Equal Credit Opportunity Act was enacted in 1974. This federal law prohibits any creditor from discriminating against an applicant on the basis of any diversity factors, such as race or religion.

Regulation 501(r)

Regulation 501(r) is a set of IRS requirements that charitable hospitals must abide by to maintain their tax-exempt status.

Patient Anti-Dumping

Formally called the Emergency Medical Treatment and Active Labor Act (EMTALA), **Patient Anti-Dumping** is a federal statute that aims to prohibit the refusal to treat potential patients who would otherwise be unable to pay at hospitals participating in Medicare with dedicated emergency departments. Congress enacted the act to try and put a stop to the practice that was becoming increasingly popular wherein a hospital would turn away indigent or uninsured patients, "dumping" or forcing them to seek treatment at another hospital.

Laboratory Licensing

Abbreviated CLIA, the **Clinical Laboratory Improvement Amendments** are federal standards enacted in 1988 that are applicable to all laboratory testing conducted on humans aside from clinical trials. CMS operates the CLIA program and the goal is to regulate testing so that certain standards are met, the research can be replicated, and a precise "score" of the complexity of the test is defined.

The Joint Commission's Major Roles

The Joint Commission (TJC) was founded in 1951 with the goal of continuously improving healthcare by evaluating and implementing quality and safety improvements in healthcare organizations. The Joint Commission is a not-for-profit healthcare organization accreditation agency.

Requirements of Accreditation Due to Participation in Medicare
Accreditation by TJC is required to participate in Medicare. Hospitals will be audited every 39 months and laboratories every two years. Hospitals are required to have contingency plans that address the entire facility.

The Patient Access Areas that Can Expect TJC Surveys
Most facilities do not receive notice that the Joint Commission is coming to survey the facility, and they usually occur sometime every 18 to 36 months. Patient access areas, including the front desk, will be surveyed.

Requirements for Contingency Plans
The contingency plan must be comprehensive and address personnel, communications, data, hardware and software, documentation, supplies, and space.

Patient Access Services

Patient Access Department's Primary Functions and Responsibilities

Trends in Reengineering the Patient Access Process

One of the growing trends in patient access is client-centered healthcare, which puts customer service and satisfaction at the forefront. Surveys seeking feedback 48 hours to 6 weeks post-service are becoming more commonplace and results are used to improve the process and experience for patients. Patient access is taking a more prominent, front-end role in the revenue cycle to prevent issues that occur with backend billing. Additionally, there is increased interest in developing mechanisms that reduce wait times and make the process as positive as possible.

Primary Functions of the Patient Access Department

Patient access associates, mainly the front desk staff, are designated personnel who should provide high quality customer service to all patients. This department is responsible for registering patients, checking them in, verifying insurance, answering questions, scheduling appointments, relaying messages to providers, and generally taking care of patients before and after their appointments. Billing, reviewing claims, sending chart notes to insurance companies, collecting copayments, preparing charts, refilling prescriptions, and sending referrals are among the many functions front desk staff may coordinate or perform.

Scheduling
Scheduling involves setting, changing, and canceling appointments. Insurance should be verified and benefits assessed after setting the first appointment but before the patient comes in.

Pre-Registration and Pre-Admission Testing
Particularly before hospital procedures, patients are contacted for pre-registration and pre-admission testing. Pre-registration involves verifying demographics, reviewing insurance benefits and authorizations, noting allergies, etc. Pre-admission testing often involves obtaining bloodwork and diagnostic imaging or an EKG, undergoing an interview by a surgical resident and/or anesthesiologist, and receiving clearance from the patient's primary care doctor.

Pre-Certification and Pre-Authorization
Most insurance companies require prior authorization for certain procedures outside of those in emergency situations. Proof of medical necessity may need to be furnished.

Inpatient Admitting and Outpatient Registration
This involves welcoming and checking in patients at the time they will receive care. A patient's name, date of birth, and other demographics will be collected and verified as will the planned reason for the visit.

Insurance Verification
A patient's eligibility needs to be confirmed. It is important to verify that coverage is active and that there are no restrictions or contingencies like pre-existing condition exemptions.

Financial Counseling
Patients need to be informed of the anticipated costs of their care, their insurance benefits (if any), and their personal financial responsibility. Payment options, including payment plans and timelines, should be discussed as per the policies of the healthcare agency.

The five **collection control points** are pre-admission, admission, in-house, discharge, and post-discharge. These are the points wherein collections are managed. A **deposit collection program**, when combined with pre-registration, can increase cash collections and reduce the total due at discharge, the amount in accounts receivable, and the overall financial risk and bad debt.

Affiliated Health Services
Examples of **affiliated health services** include access to a registered nurse 24/7, community-accessible telephone triage, referral services, available health information and a question/answer line, and in-house medical education programs.

Physician Direct Services
Examples of **physical direct services** include assistance for referrals for other specialists or community resources, notification of a patient's PCP if the patient is admitted, and marketing services of physicians on staff.

Case Management and Utilization Review's Roles and Responsibilities

Case Management Tasks and Responsibilities
The function of **case management** is to ensure the continuity of quality services for patients. The responsibilities of case managers include managerial responsibilities to facilitate the chain of steps in the patient's care, coordination of the various providers in the patient's care, and clinical functions related to implementing the care plan. Case managers facilitate communication among a multidisciplinary team, oversee follow-ups, eliminate unnecessary or repetitive steps, and coordinate care.

Levels of Patient Care Differentiated by Different Billing and Reimbursement Requirements

Acute Inpatient Care
Acute inpatient care, covered by Medicare Part A, is for patients requiring the highest level of care. Treatment here focuses on diagnosing and resolving serious and life-threatening conditions as quickly as possible.

Observation
Observation care includes a defined set of clinically-appropriate services applied to patients who present to the emergency department but then require considerable monitoring or treatment (usually up to 48 hours) before their providers can determine whether the patient can be discharged or should be admitted.

Completing the NOTICE Act's Mandated Medicare Outpatient Observation Notice (MOON)
The **MOON** informs Medicare beneficiaries when the services they are receiving are considered outpatient instead of inpatient, and when they are receiving observation services.

Outpatient Care
Medically-necessary outpatient care, like diagnostic imaging, lab work, preventative screenings, and physician visits are covered by Medicare Part B.

Long-Term Care and Custodial Care
Long-term, or custodial, care includes a variety of services and support for the personal care needs of the patient, such as activities of daily living. Because it is not medical care, most long-term care is not covered by Medicare.

Skilled Nursing Facilities (SNFs)
Skilled nursing care in a SNF is covered by Medicare Part A for homebound patients and can include things like a semi-private room, occupational or physical therapy, and ambulance transport.

Hospice and Respite Care
Provided in a patient's home or inpatient hospice facilities, **hospice care** is for those with terminal illnesses and includes things like medical services, medical supplies and equipment, and physical and occupational therapy. It is covered by Medicare Part A.

Home Healthcare
Certain services like part-time or intermittent **home health** or skilled nursing care and physical and occupational therapy may be covered by Medicare Part A and/or Part B for homebound patients who do not need skilled nursing care more often than part time or intermittently.

Office Care
Medicare Part B covers medical and mental health office visits.

Knowledge of Consent

Forms Used to Give Consent
Informed consent grants permission for the medical provider or facility to administer the proposed treatment or procedure. There are different consent forms, such as general ones, which give permission to treat (and might be signed by all new patients at a practice), or specific ones, which explicitly grant permission for a designated procedure, such as a colonoscopy, CT scan, HIV testing, or a hip replacement.

Different Types of Consent
Within the medical field, the two types of consent are **expressed** and **implied**. The following details the variations of each:

- **Actual or Expressed Consent**: Actual or expressed consent is written and signed or verbal consent by the patient or their representative.

- **Implied Consent (In Fact)**: Consent is silent but the patient implies their consent by complying.

- **Implied Consent (By Law)**: In situations where a patient is taken to the emergency room and is unconscious, it is legal to assume consent and treat the patient.

- **Informed Consent**: In order to be considered informed consent, the provider must have discussed the treatment options and given the patient the opportunity to ask questions, the decision to undergo the treatment must be made by the patient, and there is a formal record of the agreed-upon decision.

Emancipation

Emancipated minors are free from parental control and can make their own healthcare decisions. An emancipated minor has fathered or given birth to a child, does not need parental guidance or financial support, and is of a certain age.

Medical Records' Guidelines, Characteristics, and Amendments

Medical records are legal documents that must be accurate, complete, and detailed. They should be stored in safe areas where they are protected from unauthorized use, loss, and destruction by water, insects, theft, etc. With proper authorization provided by the patient or their legal representative, they can be faxed between healthcare facilities. Any falsification of a medical record can result in immediate disciplinary action including civil action and termination of employment. There are rules and policies governing handwritten entries.

The only people that can make an entry in a patient's medical record are the treating and/or attending physician, a registered nurse or nurse practitioner, a physician assistant, and a student hailing from an accredited program in health sciences who is under the direct supervision of a clinical instructor.

Verbal/Phone Orders

Verbal or telephone orders, which can be accepted by registered nurses or physician extenders (PAs, nurse practitioners, etc.), must contain the date and time the order was received, the patient's name and status, the order as stated verbatim, and the full name and role of the person documenting the order.

Advance Beneficiary Notices' (ABNs) Purpose, Causative Events, Completion, and Retention

Also called a notice of noncoverage, an ABN is used as a way to avoid the need to write off claims deemed "not reasonable or necessary" by Medicare. It states that the provider anticipates the service or item will not be covered by Medicare. The provider gives the beneficiary the ABN prior to delivering a service that will likely not meet the requirements of medical necessity. The reason that Medicare denial is likely is included on the ABN. An ABN is to be retained five years after the date of service, even if the beneficiary refused the care or refused to sign the ABN. ABNs are not to be used for services or items billed under Medicare Part C or Part D.

Necessary Modifiers When Billing with an ABN
There are four main modifiers used with ABNs:

- GA: used with mandatory ABNs
- GX: used with voluntary ABNs
- GY: used with services or items statutorily excluded or not considered a Medicare benefit
- GZ: used with services or items that are expected to be denied on the grounds that they are considered not reasonable or necessary

Definitive Versus Non-Definitive Local Coverage Determinations (LCDs) and National Coverage Determinations (NCDs)

LCDs and NCDs list and describe specific diagnoses and procedure codes for definitive diagnoses. They may also include signs and symptoms that indicate the need for the service or item rendered. With a non-definitive diagnosis, the LCD or NCD offers possible coverage options, but not specific codes or symptoms that will or will not be covered.

Secondary Payer Provisions for Medicare

Using the Initial Enrollment Questionnaire (IEQ)

The **Initial Enrollment Questionnaire** (IEQ) is a form for individuals who are newly eligible for Medicare. The form is mailed three months prior to the date an individual will become entitled to enroll.

Using the MSP Questionnaire

The **Medicare Secondary Payer** (MSP) questionnaire includes questions about accidents and employment to help determine the appropriate coordination of benefits.

Using the Common Working File

Patients' Medicare eligibility and utilization data is included in the **Common Working File**. It serves as a national registry of enrolled individuals so eligibility, benefits period, deductibles, effective date, patient's relationship to insured, birthday, etc. can be verified.

Calculating Important Patient Access Metrics

- **Average Length of Stay**: The total number of patient days is dived by the number of discharges.

Midnight Census: This value, which is the number of patients in the hospital at a given time, is found by subtracting any discharges from the census count at the previous midnight and adding any admissions, followed by adding or subtracting any status changes.

Average Daily Census: The mean number of inpatients over a given time period. It is found by adding the total number of patient days during that time period and dividing it by the number of days in that time period.

Percentage of Occupancy: This is calculated by dividing the census of the day by the number of available licensed beds. It uses bed capacity to determine the ratio of actual patient days to the maximum.

Hospital and Clinic Billing

Insurance Types and Payer Types

Medicare

Coverage and Criteria for Medical Necessity
Coverage must be active in order for medically-necessary services to be billable. For a service or item to be considered medically necessary, it must be shown to be safe and effective for the patient's diagnosis or symptoms, rather than being solely provided for convenience.

Part A Deductibles, Coinsurance, and Copayments
Part A, hospital insurance, helps pay for inpatient hospitalization that is medically necessary, or care in a skilled nursing facility after a 3-day hospital stay, home healthcare, or hospice care. The deductible is paid once per illness or benefit period, which is considered to begin when the beneficiary enters the hospital or skilled nursing facility and ends when discharged. Patients are responsible for their deductible, coinsurance, and copayment.

Part B Deductibles, Coinsurance, and Copayments
Medicare Part B provides partial coverage for medically-necessary office and physician services and outpatient medical care. Signing up for Part B coverage is only possible in the 7-month window of time that begins three months prior to the beneficiary turning 65. After this period, the beneficiary can sign up, but monthly premiums will be higher. Patients usually have 20% coinsurance fees and an annual deductible.

Part B Preventive Services and Other Service
Part B helps cover outpatient medical and surgical services, physician services, medical supplies, therapies (physical, occupational, and speech/language), clinical laboratory services, facility fees at ambulatory surgery center for approved procedures, outpatient mental healthcare, and durable medical equipment. Covered preventative services include things like bone density testing, colorectal cancer screening, diabetes screening and self-management education, glaucoma screening, mammograms, certain vaccinations (such as hepatitis B and C), prostate cancer screening, annual wellness exams, HIV and hepatitis screening, medical nutrition therapy, cardiovascular and AAA screening, smoking cessation therapy, and screening for depression and other behavioral health services. Other services that are covered include therapeutic shoes for patients with diabetes, eyeglasses, neck and back braces, diagnostic imaging, prostheses, dialysis treatment, and emergency care.

Items Not Covered by Part A or Part B in the Original Medicare Plan
The following are services or items not covered by Part A or Part B in the original Medicare plan:

- Acupuncture
- Cosmetic Surgeries
- Routine dental services
- Hearing aids and exams
- Custodial care
- Foot orthotics
- Services needed when traveling internationally (in most cases)
- Services for injuries incurred in a war
- Certain diabetic supplies like syringes

- Routine eye care and glasses when the patient does not have a related disease
- Routine foot care
- Physicals that are not wellness visits
- Certain vaccines
- Any deductible, premium, copayment, or coinsurance are also not covered

Part C and Types of Medicare Advantage Plans
Medicare Part C, Medicare Advantage Plans, are private insurance companies that Medicare has approved to offer managed care coverage that abide by certain rules. These may be HMOs, PPOs, private Fee-for-Service plans, Special Needs Plans, and Medicare Medical Savings Accounts.

The Purpose of Part D
Part D provides prescription drug coverage.

Medicare Participating Physician Program
Medicare Participating Physician Program allows providers to accept Medicare's assignment of benefits so that payment is remitted to the provider and not the patient.

Health Insurance Claim Numbers
When the health insurance claim number starts with A, six digits follow. When it starts with a number, the first nine characters are digits and the last character is an alpha or alphanumeric suffix that classifies the beneficiary. When it starts with MA, PA, WA, or WCA, six digits follow.

HICN Suffixes
There are many health insurance claim number suffixes for Medicare that help denote more about the claim. Some examples are as follows:

- A = an individual, aged 65 or older, who earns wages
- B = aged 65 or older wife
- B1 = aged 65 or older husband
- C1 = youngest child
- F3 = stepfather
- W = disabled widow

Medigap
Medigap, also called **Medicare supplemental insurance**, is a private health insurance purchased by some Medicare beneficiaries to fill Original Medicare Plan (not Part D) coverage gaps, such as deductibles, coinsurance, and copayments), and, in some cases, benefits Medicare doesn't cover, such as emergency medical services needed during international travel.

Medicaid
Funded through a partnership between the federal and state governments, **Medicaid** is a health insurance program for those who meet certain low-income requirements or have specific chronic conditions. Individual states can set eligibility guidelines, payment schedules, and benefits. **Dual eligibility** refers to people who are eligible for both Medicare Part A and/or B as well as some form of Medicaid coverage.

Workers' Compensation
Employees who are injured on the job may have coverage for their work-related injuries from their employer. A claim number is needed for the case.

Tricare
Active and retired members of the U.S. uniformed services are eligible for **Tricare**, a regionally-managed healthcare program, as are their families and survivors.

Non-Availability Statement (NAS)
A non-Military Treatment Facility must provide this to a Tricare or Tricare Extra beneficiary prior to any non-emergent inpatient services.

Children's Health Insurance Program (CHIP)
Administered by states but funded by the federal and state governments together, CHIP is a program intended to make health insurance more affordable for parents whose income and assets exceed those of Medicaid eligibility but are insufficient to purchase private insurance. Certain procedures must be covered under CHIP like immunizations, well child care, inpatient and outpatient hospital services, and x-ray and laboratory services.

Self-Insurance
Regulated through ERISA, in self-insurance situations, third parties are paid to administer benefits from a fund into which a company has paid premiums.

Insurance Payer Contracts
Physicians and facilities negotiate contracts with insurance payers to establish covered services and fees.

Properly Coordinating Benefits

Medicare as Primary vs. Secondary Insurance
If Medicare is primary, it is the first insurance billed. If it is secondary, the primary insurance is billed first and any remaining on the claim is billed to Medicare.

Those for Whom Medicare is Secondary
Medicare may be a secondary payer when the beneficiary is aged 65 or older and is working for an employer that offers group health insurance or has an employed spouse of any age whose employer offers group health insurance. Medicare may also be secondary for those with the following:

- End-stage renal disease
- Those who are under the age of 65 but disabled and covered by a group health plan
- Those who are getting care paid for by no-fault claims or Workers' Compensation or the U.S. Department of Veteran's Affairs
- Those getting care covered via the Black Lung Benefit Act.

Conditional Payments
Medicare will make a payment on a claim in certain instances when another payer is responsible, but prompt payment is not anticipated (typically, payment is not expected to occur within 120 days after the claim date). This prevents the beneficiary from needing to make an out-of-pocket payment.

Other Factors that Determine the Coordination of Benefits

Some examples of things to consider concerning the coordination of benefits include, but are not limited to, the following:

- Medicaid is the "payer of last resort." Aside from the Indian Health Service, no plan will ever be secondary to Medicaid.

- Federal law mandates Tricare be the last payer on a claim with just a few exceptions, such as Medicaid and the Indian Health Service.

- In the case of accidents or injuries, any casualty, liability, or property insurance should be billed as the primary payer.

Role of a Coordination of Benefits Contractor

While a **coordination of benefits contractor** doesn't process any claims for a provider, he or she does help collect, manage, report, and disseminate information regarding coordination of benefits. COB contractors administer the IEQ and help perform MSP investigations on claims. They also have a key role in helping providers determine primary and secondary payer status and employment changes.

Transaction Code Sets

ICD-10
ICD stands for the International Classification of Diseases. The **10** denotes the 10th edition. ICD-10 codes are used to express the patient's diagnoses and any inpatient procedures.

CPT and HCPCS Level I and Level II
CPT, **Current Procedural Terminology**, and HCPCS, the **Healthcare Common Procedure Coding System**, are systems of codes used to describe outpatient procedures. CPT codes are commonly used for services rendered by physicians and healthcare professionals. HCPCS Level 1 codes contain the system of CPT codes. CMS assigns HCPCS Level II codes, which contain five digits preceded by a letter (A through V), to services, products, and supplies not included in the system of CPT codes, such as prostheses and ambulance services.

Evaluation & Management (E&M) Levels
Evaluation & Management (E&M) levels refer to the level of care, based on seven identified components, that a provider assigns to each patient based on the entire process of evaluating and treating that patient. The levels relate to the time spent with the patient and the complexity of treating him or her. Reimbursement fees are associated with the level of care.

HCPCS and CPT Modifiers
Modifiers are used to denote the alteration of a service in some way that impacts the reimbursement. Attaching one of these two-character alphanumeric or numeric codes to a defined HCPCS or CPT code alerts CMS that the service was changed in some way but there is no other existing code that accurately describes what was performed.

Different Payment Methodologies

Diagnosis-Related Group (DRG)
In the **Diagnosis-Related Group** (DRG) classification system, patients are grouped by criteria such as primary diagnosis, treatment plan, and age. There is a set reimbursement fee for hospitals treating patients in a given DRG under the prospective payment system; their specific treatment costs do not affect the payment.

Ambulatory Payment Classification (APC)
Ambulatory Payment Classification is the U.S. government's way of paying for outpatient services for Medicare. Required elements to assign an APC include HCPCS and CPT codes, E&M codes, ICD-10 codes, and where the service was rendered. Examples of packaged services are anesthesia, time in the recovery room, observation, supplies and contrast agents, and implantable devices. Certain hospitals are exempt, such as cancer hospitals, critical access hospitals, and others.

Critical Access Hospital (CAH)
Critical Access Hospitals (CAHs) have fewer than 26 beds and exist in rural areas, at least a designated minimum distance from other hospitals. They must offer emergency services 24/7. Reimbursement is different; they are paid by Medicare based on allowable costs calculated from the cost report from the previous year and paid by other payers based on whatever contract terms have been negotiated.

Resource Utilization Group (RUG)
The **Resource Utilization Group** (RUG) system helps Medicare decide the payment rate for a service.

Capitation
Although submitting claims is still required, **capitation** is a payment method by which providers receive a predetermined payment per patient for a specific length of time. The amount covers all care during that time period, regardless as to the actual charges or services rendered.

Per Diem
Per diem is a payment method where providers receive a set amount per day for the inpatient's care no matter what care was needed.

Determining Value of Services

Resource Based Relative Value Scale (RBRVS)
The **resource-based relative value scale** helps provide uniformity to compensation by considering the relative value of services rendered by physicians across the country.

Three Major Elements Comprising RBRVS
Three major elements of comprising RBRVS are the reimbursement schedule for physicians (which is based on the Relative Value Unit), the rate Medicare's expenditures for services furnished by physicians increased due to Medicare Volume Performance Standards, and limits on charges that beneficiaries will incur from non-participating physicians.

Three Relative Value Units (RVUs)
The three relative value units associated with calculating a payment under the Medicare Prospective Payment System (MPPS) are the following:

- The amount of work required
- Fees for professional liability insurance
- The expense of malpractice insurance for the practice

Usual, Customary, and Reasonable (UCR)
Usual, customary, and reasonable is the amount consumers pay for medical services in a certain location based on what other providers charge for the same or similar medical service in the same area. The **UCR** is used by third party payers to set their reimbursement fees for services.

Chargemaster

Chargemaster Purpose and Use
A practice's **chargemaster**, or fee schedule, is an exhaustive list of all billable procedures, which is used to prepare a patient's statement. The listed rates are usually significantly inflated compared to the true cost, but these listed costs serve as a starting value for reimbursement negotiations.

Chargemaster Elements
A typical chargemaster includes all possible medical services, equipment, medications, diagnostic procedures, supplies, etc. and an associated cost for each listed item. It also includes the supplier and cost for items on inventory. Department numbers, revenue codes, CPT/HCPCS codes and modifiers, ledger numbers, and charge amounts and descriptions are all included on the chargemaster.

Chargemaster Review Best Practices
Because CMS is subject to change its rules every quarter, it's critical that the chargemaster is reviewed at least as frequently so that it remains accurate. It is important to have a review procedure in place to compare the chargemaster with CMS rules and other rules and regulations that may have changed with private insurances as well. It helps to have a designated person to review the chargemaster and keep it updated and accurate because experience and continuity can be built, reducing errors and improving efficiency of the review process itself.

Common Billing Forms

Superbill
Used during patient encounters, the **superbill** is an invoice form for providers to mark procedures rendered during the appointment so that an appropriate bill can be prepared.

UB-04 (and 837I)
CMS requires the **UB-04** (and **837I**) claim form from hospitals (inpatient and outpatient), skilled nursing facilities, community mental health centers, comprehensive rehab facilities, and home health professionals.

CMS 1500 (and 5010A1/837P)
Physician and professional services are documented on the **CMS 1500** claim form. No more than six lines of services should be included per form.

Itemized Statement
Every service or item posted to a patient's account, the **itemized statement** includes the date each service was rendered, a description and code for the service, the amount charged to the account, the estimated insurance reimbursement and patient responsibility, and the total on the account.

Data Mailer
A **data mailer** is a free-form statement generated by the billing system that reports that status of a patient's account and can be used to bill the patient for any outstanding balance.

Explanation of Benefits (EOB) or Remittance Advice (RA)
Policyholders and providers receive an **explanation of benefits** (EOB) from the insurance company. It details the patient's benefits for a certain service, the reimbursement from the insurance, and the patient's estimated out-of-pocket cost. **Remittance Advice** (RAs) explain the rejections, denials, and payments on a claim to a facility. They are typically sent to the provider, rather than the policyholder, and contain more detailed information about the breakdown of charges. The following lists the information typically included on an EOB:

- The patient's name, provider's name, and payer's name
- Details regarding the performed services
- The fees the doctor or facility billed and what the plan allows
- Reductions to the billed fees based on what the insurance will pay
- The patient's responsibility
- Any other fee adjustments and reasons are included on an EOB

The description of services rendered on an EOB can alert a patient to what their doctor billed for the care rendered. Patients can identify fraudulent or abusive charges and upcoding, among others.

Mandatory Filing Requirements and Exceptions

Healthcare providers are required to submit the appropriate claims when delivering a covered service or item to a Medicare beneficiary. This is necessary to avoid a Civil Monetary Penalty of up to $10,000 per violation, unless an approved exception is in place. Exceptions include situations where Medicare is secondary, the patient failed to provide information about the primary insurance, the care was rendered internationally, the patient signed an ABN stating not to bill for the services, the service is not covered by Medicare, or the provider is disbarred or electively opted out of the Medicare program.

Billing Timeframes and Their Importance

Timely Filing for Medicare
Claims for Medicare must be billed no later than 12 months after the date of service, which is determined by the "From" date. Timely filing is crucial to avoid penalties, unprocessed claims, and loss of revenue.

Medicare 3-Day Rule
The **Medicare 3-day rule** mandates that all diagnostic or outpatient services associated with the primary admitting diagnosis that occurred within three days before the patient was admitted to the hospital are bundled with the inpatient services on the Medicare claim. The 3-Day Rule applies to any diagnostic or outpatient service. The provision does not apply to ambulance services and outpatient services that are not diagnostic in nature, are not related to the primary diagnosis for which the patient gets admitted, or occurred more than three days before admission are not bundled on the claim.

Hospitals Subject to the 1-Day Rule Instead of the 3-Day Rule
Psychiatric, rehabilitation, children's, critical access, cancer, non-PPS, international, and long-term care hospitals are not subject to the 3-Day Rule. These facilities are subject to the 1-Day Rule instead.

Billing for Services Unrelated to the Inpatient Admission
Services that were furnished that were unrelated to the primary diagnosis for which the patient ultimately was admitted are not bundled together.

Electronic Claim Processing Considerations and Important Medicare Edits

Methods to Originate and Transfer Electronic Claims
Electronic claims can be transferred via manual entry, computer download, from CPU to CPU, or via tape transfer.

Benefits and Drawbacks of Electronic Billing
Electronic billing offers environmental benefits of less paper. It also allows for a faster payment floor, faster submission to the payer, reduces staffing resources and clerical intervention, and more easily permits follow-up. It is also easy to furnish a proof of receipts and billing reports and can result in higher interest payments when payments are delayed.

Drawbacks include the inability to send attachments, the potential difficulty with payer, acceptance, issues with uploading and downloading, challenges regarding backward integration, and unavailable or inflexible vendor reporting.

Medicare Edits
Edits to claims can be carried out via Medicare Code Editor (MCE). Medicare grants 45 days to submit a corrected claim.

Three Basic Types of Edits
MCE is used for three basic types of edits:

- **Clinical edits**: Deal with issues of consistency or clinical reasonability of procedural and diagnostic services billed

- **Coverage edits**: Deal with issues regarding the type of procedure rendered for the patient and if it is covered or not

- **Code edits**: Deal with incorrect use of ICD-10 codes

Clean Claims
A **clean claim** will pass the Common Working File edits and is processed electronically. It should not have been generated at a post-payment time. It should include all medical notes, as necessary, attached to the initial claim as per the instructions. Clean claims also do not require Medicare to contact the provider or beneficiary if the claim is investigated.

National Correct Coding Initiative (NCCI)
National Correct Coding Initiative (NCCI) establishes medical billing standards, promotes correct coding procedures, and aims to reduce coding errors. It identifies codes that are more likely to be subject to fraud and abuse, as well as those that should be bundled together on one claim.

Medically Unlikely Edits (MUE)

Medically Unlikely Edits (MUEs) were developed by CMS to reduce errors on paid Part B claims. They place maximums on units of service a provider can bill for each CPT code per patient on a single day of service.

Guidelines that Ensure Compliance Plans are Effective

OIG's Seven Elements of a Compliance Plan

Compliance plans are designed to assist providers in avoiding, identifying, and fixing areas of noncompliance with Medicare's rules. The elements include policies and procedures that are written clearly, auditing and monitoring processes, training and education that is appropriate and effective, lines of communication that are open, standards that are enforced and disciplinary procedures that are well-publicized, a designated compliance committee and a compliance officer in place, and procedures by which offenses are addressed and corrective. Compliance plans must comply with all laws and regulations.

Credit and Collections

Terms Related to Credit and Collections

Charity Care: Healthcare services rendered for free or at a discounted rate to those who demonstrate a designated level of financial need.

Indigent: Indigents are those who lack any means to pay for medical services and are also ineligible for any public assistance program.

Bad Debt: The result of the extension of credit, bad debt is an account that is considered uncollectable, such as those from patients who skip or file bankruptcy without assets or who default from payment arrangements.

Judgment: This is a claim against someone who is in debt. The claim is legally validated by the court. It can be used to obtain a lien because the creditor has a legal right to collect the debt.

Lien: Usually arising out of debt, a lien is a recorded claim against personal or real property. In cases where that property is sold, proceeds are paid to the creditor.

Tort Liability: An injury or wrongdoing that one person causes another due to a breach of legal duty is considered tort liability.

Statute of Limitations: This is the length of time by which a claim must be collected. Otherwise, it is considered paid or satisfied. When this statute of limitations expires, legal proceedings can no longer be initiated.

Elements in an Effective Collection Policy

Collection policies should be written and formalized, and include elements such as minimum acceptable payments, the admissions and public relations policies, how follow-up is conducted and by whom, practices concerning discounts and interest (if applicable), a description of the procedure to verify the responsible party, the age that an account is written off as bad debt, and the processes for error and complaint handling.

Bankruptcy

Bankruptcy, a legal proceeding, occurs when the debts of the responsible party well exceed their assets, and there is no reason to believe repayment will be possible.

Types

Chapter 7 bankruptcy applies to individuals and companies who, based on their income, cannot pay their debts except for exempt property as defined by state laws. The assets held by the debtor, aside from property exempt according to state laws, are auctioned to repay the debt.

Often called *reorganization*, **Chapter 11 bankruptcy** grants a reprieve from immediately satisfying claims to a distressed business so that they can continue to operate and work out a plan for repayment. If a debtor has more than 11 creditors, with at least three with claims greater than $5,000, or has fewer than 12 creditors but one has a claim of $10,775 or more, Chapter 7 or Chapter 11 bankruptcy is forced.

Chapter 12 bankruptcy is only for family farmers who have a regular annual income that might permit the debtor to repay the debt.

Individuals who want to repay their debt and have a regular income but cannot yet pay the claims are subject to a **Chapter 13 bankruptcy**. The court can supervise and protect the debtor while he or she proposes and fulfills a long-term repayment plan.

Effect on the Collection Process and Potential Outcomes

When a patient or responsible party claims bankruptcy, the practice or creditor should confirm the bankruptcy. After receipt of the bankrupt's notices, collection activity should be ceased, and third-party collections agencies should be notified.

In the **discharge of debtor** notice, the patient or guarantor is released from the financial responsibility of the balance on the account. With the application of a transaction code on the bankruptcy petition, the account balance is written off so long as it was incurred before the petition. In a **dismissal** court filing, the court rejects the bankruptcy.

Requirements for Counseling Sessions

An individual or business that plans to file for bankruptcy must obtain credit counseling at a government-approved organization within six months prior to filing.

How to Decide Who is the Responsible Party in a Given Scenario

The responsible party is often the adult patient or the subscriber on the health insurance, even if the injuries incurred are the result of another party's negligence. Depending on the state, the spouses may be eligible for one another's debt, even if the spouse who was the patient died. With minors, both parents, if they are jointly and fully responsible for their child, are equally responsible, even if they are divorced. Even if an authorization for emergency services is not obtained, the responsible party is still obligated to pay. Lastly, the estate of a deceased patient can be the responsible party.

Advantages of a Courtesy Discharge

Courtesy discharges can improve traffic flow, patient-hospital relations, and billing accuracy. It can also reduce the number of staff needed at times where the number of discharges is high.

Delays and Stalls from Third Party Payers

Common delays and stalls from third party payers include the following:

- Failure to receive the bill from the practice
- The need to receive and review medical notes or the record
- Incorrect information (demographics, insurance details, etc.) was provided by the insured patient
- An authorization or a referral was not obtained or is not on file
- The claim was not filed in a timely manner
- Problems with the coding
- The association of the claim with a pre-existing condition
- Issues with coordination of benefits
- Billing an ineligible code

There can also be stop loss issues and adjudication delays on the administrative side with the third-party payer.

Common Methods and Practices of Debt Collection

In-House Collections

When collections are conducted in-house, it is the responsibility of the practice to contact patients and third party payers who owe money and get them to remit payments.

Purpose and Importance of Following Up with Third Party Payers

Third party payers, which are public or private organizations that insure or cover medical expenses on behalf of a patient, do not always remit payments in a timely manner. Moreover, billing errors can result in non-payments. To prevent delays in receiving revenue owed for billable services, in-house collection agents should regularly follow up with third party payers to recoup payments for unpaid claims.

Strategies for Collection Efforts

To optimize the chances of recovering debt from patients and third-party payers, in-house collection agents can employ strategies such as establishing the expectation of payment at the time the service is rendered, informing the patient of anticipated costs at the time of scheduling, offering payment options and payment plans, making payment convenient with online patient portals, etc.

Steps for Making Collection Calls

Employing a set of steps that help organize and streamline collection calls can result in better customer relations and more successful outcomes. The following steps are often helpful:

- Identify the patient by name.
- Identify the provider or facility and the collector should identify himself or herself by name and role.
- Offer all payment methods, but request payment in full.
- Provide the patient time to think and respond.
- Identify if a problem exists in receiving the payment and how it might be solved.
- Make arrangements for payment.
- Document the call and the outcome.

Collection Agencies

Some practices outsource the process of collections to dedicated collections agencies. This strategy is often most successful in cases of hard-to-collect debt and it can remove pressure from the billing staff. However, it is expensive, often costing 20 to 50% of the sum collected.

Skip Tracing

Skip tracing identifies people who owe money but whose contact information is incorrect, not up-to-date, or cannot be readily found. Practices can hire skip tracers to track down the debtors.

Types of Skips

There are three main types of skips: unintentional, intentional, and false. In an **unintentional skip**, the individual has moved and forgotten to notify creditors; usually, a forwarding address is available. Like the name implies, in an **intentional skip**, the person moves or changes their name without notifying creditors or providing a forwarding address. The debtor may also have purposely provided false information. In a **false skip**, a clerical error has occurred, usually when registering the patient.

Resources to Trace Skips
There are different resources and databases like credit reports, criminal background checks, public tax information, loyalty cards, vehicle registration records, and utility bills that skip tracers may use.

Standard Counting Principles for Cashiers

Cashiers are responsible for operating the cash register in an error-free fashion, processing payments in a variety of forms, maintaining a correct cash balance in the register, sorting and wrapping coins and paper currency, and interacting with patients.

Calculating Common Metrics Related to Collection

Average Daily Revenue
Average daily revenue is calculated by dividing the total revenue from the accounting period by the number of days in the period.

Average Days of Revenue in Accounts Receivable (ADRR)
ADRR is an estimate of how long it will take to collect the accounts receivable. It is calculated by dividing the total amount from the billing period in accounts receivable by the total sales during that time, and then multiplying this by the number of days in the billing period.

Practice Questions

1. What are the two primary types of advance directives?
    a. An organ donation card and a Durable Power of Attorney for Healthcare
    b. A Durable Power of Attorney for Healthcare and a Living Will
    c. A Living Will and a "Do Not Resuscitate" order
    d. A "Do Not Resuscitate" order and an organ donation card

2. Under the ACA, at least how often do tax-exempt hospitals need to conduct a CHNA as one of the criteria for retaining their tax-exempt status?
    a. Annually
    b. Every other year
    c. Every three years
    d. Every five years

3. Which of the following best describes a dual eligible beneficiary?
    a. Someone entitled to Medicare Part A and/or Part B, and Medicaid benefits of some form.
    b. Someone entitled to Medicare Part A and Medicare Part B.
    c. Someone entitled to Medicare Part A and/or Part B, and Medicaid Part C and/or Part D.
    d. Someone entitled to Medicare Part A and/or Part B, and Tricare.

4. Which of the following is NOT one of the RVUs associated with calculating a payment under the MPPS?
    a. The amount of work required
    b. Professional liability insurance fees
    c. Malpractice insurance expenses
    d. Nonparticipating providers' charge limits

5. Which of the following forms would a skilled nursing facility use when billing Medicare?
    a. UB-04
    b. CMS 1500
    c. 5010A1
    d. 837P

Answer Explanations

1. B: The most common types of advanced directives are the Durable Power of Attorney for Healthcare and a Living Will. An advance directive gives permission to a specified person should an individual become unable to make their own healthcare decisions. Do Not Resuscitate orders, organ and tissue donation decisions, and the use of dialysis or ventilators are examples of things that may be included on an advanced directive, but they are not types of advance directions.

2. C: Under the ACA, tax-exempt hospitals must conduct and implement a CHNA (Community Health Needs Assessment) at least once every three years.

3. A: A dual eligible person is entitled to both Medicare Part A and/or Part B and some form of Medicaid. In these cases, Medicare would be the primary payer because Medicaid is always the last payer, with the exception of those with Indian Health Service.

4. D: Nonparticipating providers' charge limits are not associated with calculating a payment under the MPPS. Revenue Value Limits (RVUs) affect payments under the Medicare Prospective Payment System. The amount of work required and expenses related to carrying professional liability insurance and malpractice insurance for the practice are considered.

5. A: CMS requires skilled nursing facilities, hospitals, community mental health centers, comprehensive rehab facilities, and home health professionals to use the UB-04 or electronic 8371. The other forms listed are all versions of the form used for physicians and professional services.

Greetings!

First, we would like to give a huge "thank you" for choosing us and this study guide for your CRCS exam. We hope that it will lead you to success on this exam and for your years to come.

Our team has tried to make your preparations as thorough as possible by covering all of the topics you should be expected to know. In addition, our writers attempted to create practice questions identical to what you will see on the day of your actual test. We have also included many test-taking strategies to help you learn the material, maintain the knowledge, and take the test with confidence.

We strive for excellence in our products, and if you have any comments or concerns over the quality of something in this study guide, please send us an email so that we may improve.

As you continue forward in life, we would like to remain alongside you with other books and study guides in our library. We are continually producing and updating study guides in several different subjects. If you are looking for something in particular, all of our products are available on Amazon. You may also send us an email!

Sincerely,
APEX Test Prep
info@apexprep.com